KidLit

What's So Great About Shakespeare?

A Biography of William Shakespeare Just for Kids!

Sam Rogers

KidLit-O Books
www.kidlito.com

© 2014. All Rights Reserved.

Cover Image © dedMazay - Fotolia.com

Table of Contents

ABOUT KIDCAPS 3

INTRODUCTION 5

CHAPTER 1: SHAKESPEARE'S EARLY LIFE..........11

CHAPTER 2: THE CAREER OF WILLIAM
SHAKESPEARE 24

CHAPTER 3: THE LATE LIFE OF WILLIAM
SHAKESPEARE 40

CHAPTER 4: WHAT'S SO GREAT ABOUT
SHAKESPEARE? 49

About KidCaps

KidLit-O is an imprint of BookCaps™ that is just for kids! Each month BookCaps will be releasing several books in this exciting imprint. Visit are website or like us on Facebook to see more!

To add your name to our mailing list, visit this link: http://www.kidlito.com/mailing-list.html

[1] Image source: http://upload.wikimedia.org/wikipedia/commons/3/31/William_Sha kespeare_1609.jpg

Introduction

William Shakespeare peeked from behind the curtain to catch a glimpse of the audience that was already in their seats waiting for the show to begin. Today, Shakespeare and his troupe of actors were going to put on a special performance of his hit play *The Merchant of Venice*, and the whole team of performers had worked long and hard to make sure that every detail of the show came out perfectly. Although Shakespeare himself would only be playing a small role in the play, he still felt that this performance before this important audience would be a special opportunity to showcase his writing talents.

King James I had invited Shakespeare's acting troupe "The King's Men" to his palace for a private performance, and this meant that the actors had to make some adjustments to their play. The men normally performed their shows in a theater they had built for themselves – the Globe Theater – but because the King insisted on seeing the play in his palace the actors would have to use a different stage. There were a thousand little details to worry about, including different ropes for raising and lowering the curtain, a different balcony for the musicians to sit in and the actors to use, different locations for the actors to enter and exit the stage, and different methods for creating the special effects of the show.

Although these details worried Shakespeare each time he performed in the Court, today he smiled as he reminded himself that at least the audience in King James' Court would probably be a little better behaved than they would be at the Globe. At least Shakespeare wouldn't have to worry about getting hit in the face with a piece of rotten cabbage.

The actors who were going to play the parts of Antonio and Salarino were already in costume and their makeup had been applied. They were standing nervously at stage right and rehearsing their lines for the first scene under their breath. All the actors in the group of travelling performers had appeared before royalty in the past, but that never stopped them from being nervous.

Despite having spent the better part of two decades in theaters, Shakespeare himself had double and triple-checked all of the details for tonight's performance, and over the sound of his beating heart he found himself praying that he wouldn't look like a fool in front of the most powerful man in the world.

The banner above the stage unfurled, signaling that the show was about to begin. The conversation out in the audience chamber quieted, and the King and his wife smiled at each other as the two actors walked out onto the stage. The actor playing Antonio, the Merchant of Venice the play was named for, began reciting his lines in the hushed room, complaining that he was troubled but didn't know why:

> In sooth, I know not why I am so sad:
> It wearies me; you say it wearies you;
> But how I caught it, found it, or came by it,
> What stuff 'tis made of, whereof it is born,
> I am to learn;
> And such a want-wit sadness makes of me,
> That I have much ado to know myself.

Shakespeare smiled as he watched the scene unfold. His fellow actors were doing splendidly so far, and with relief he felt that his heart finally began to slow down. Turning to walk behind the scenery to the section where the costumes were hanging, Shakespeare pulled his costume from off the rack and began to get dressed. As he fastened the clasps on his clothing, he reflected on what had brought him to this point, to the moment where professional actors were reciting the lines that he had written before the King and Queen of England.

For some 20 years William had practiced his art as an actor, poet, and playwright. At first, his friends and family were embarrassed by the career that he had chosen, but now here he was in the palace of the King and performing a show at the personal request of this ruler of England. There had been many ups and downs in his life and there were plenty of moments when he thought he would never succeed, but despite it all William Shakespeare had persevered - and now he had the respect and admiration of an entire nation.

William Shakespeare lived in a time called "the Golden Age of England", when rulers like Queen Elizabeth I and James I encouraged English playwrights and poets to produce new works. Both of these monarchs personally invited Shakespeare to perform for them and both gave him lots of praise. Back when actors were not taken seriously and certainly weren't respected in the community, Shakespeare got the attention of thousands of people and made them listen to what he had to say.

Today, nearly 400 years after his death, students and theatergoers alike still marvel at the beautiful words written by "the Bard (poet) of Avon", and professors continue to debate the ideas Shakespeare may or may not have tried to convey in his plays.

Born in a small town far away from the royal palace, this writer - with little more than a basic education -would eventually add thousands of words to the English language, would instruct Kings as to how they should act, and would calm potential civil unrest with a simple flick of his pen. His plays would make him a rich man, and even though some people today question how much writing Shakespeare actually did, there is plenty of evidence to show that the man was recognized as a genius and a superstar even during his own lifetime.

But William Shakespeare left behind very little information about his personal life and his feelings. Researchers and historians have had no choice but to try to piece together Shakespeare's life as if it were a sort of puzzle, the pieces being the few public documents and comments by people living at the same time that mention Shakespeare. With these few printed pages, researchers try and learn more about the life of this famous writer. While there are missing periods from Shakespeare's life where we can only guess where William was and what he was doing, overall there have been just enough scraps of paper to give us a clear picture of who Shakespeare was and how he lived.

The story of William Shakespeare begins with his birth on April 23, 1564. He was born to a Catholic family in a time when Queen Mary I of England was doing her best to convince the entire country to support the Catholic Church. But when Shakespeare turned 4 years old, a new Queen sat down on her throne, and under her rule Catholics (include Shakespeare's parents) would be treated very differently.

Chapter 1: Shakespeare's Early Life

Sometime between the years 1556 and 1558, a man named John Shakespeare married a young woman named Mary Arden, and within a short time this lovely couple started to have babies and to fill their large house in Stratford-upon-Avon with joy and laughter.

John Shakespeare and his family were very faithful to the Catholic Church and were happy

[2] Image source: http://en.wikipedia.org/wiki/Stratford-upon-Avon

to have a Catholic Queen sitting on England's throne. Those who disagreed with John and Mary's religion would be punished – and the Shakespeare family did not necessarily see anything wrong with this. They knew that the leader of their Church – the Pope – wanted them to obey Queen Mary. So if Mary thought that non-Catholics should be tortured and executed, then who were they to argue?

John and Mary Shakespeare eventually had eight children, but only five of them survived to be adults. Although it is sad to think of children dying so young – and of course John and Mary were sad each time one of their kids died – it wasn't terribly uncommon for families to lose several kids before they became adults. In a time before modern medicine, little kids often got sick, and when no one could find a cure for their fever or diarrhea, they died. And aside from a normal fever or a bout of stomach problems, there was an even worse threat for the Shakespeare children: the Plague. In the time of Shakespeare, one out of every three children died before they reached 10 years of age.

Diseases weren't understood very well back in Shakespeare's day, and sometimes the symptoms got mixed up and lumped together as if they were part of one disease called "the Plague". Common symptoms that indicated serious problems included high fevers, the victim's skin turning black, swelling in certain parts of the body, and quick deaths (often within just a few days of getting sick).

At the time, no one could be too sure where these diseases came from or how the disease spread from one person to another. Many years later, it was discovered that at least one of the diseases that struck Europe during the Middle Ages may have been brought over from Asia by fleas that lived on rats. These rats would climb aboard the ships that travelled from place to another, and then the fleas would jump off and start biting people, making them sick.

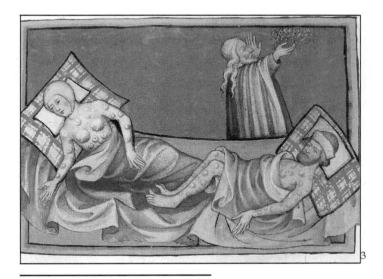

[3] Image source: http://en.wikipedia.org/wiki/Black_Death

It is also possible that the plague may have been transmitted from one person to another through sneezing and coughing. Even though modern-day scientists know a lot more about the different plagues than Shakespeare and his family did, there are still some things that we don't understand. But back then, the people in general thought that maybe God was punishing them with these terrible sicknesses, that the disease was spread by foreigners visiting England, or that wearing roses or other special mixtures on their clothing could protect them from getting sick.

It was a terrible time to grow up, and three of John and Mary's children – Joan, Mary, and Anne – died before they turned 18.

It was in this environment of constant fear, death, and uncertainty that William was born on April 23, 1564. Of his seven brothers and sisters, four of them lived into adulthood and lived lives of their own. After John and Mary had William, they had Gilbert next, then another daughter they named after their first one (Joan) before welcoming two more boys to the family, Richard and Edmund.

The Shakespeares lived together in a modest-sized house in the quiet town of Stratford-upon-

Avon. John worked in leather, making clothing items like gloves, and dabbled in different investments throughout the years, including real estate. Later on, John also served as a politician in Stratford-upon-Avon, serving on City Council as an "Alderman" and later working as a "High Bailiff", or what is now known as a Mayor.

For her part, Mary focused on raising the children – four energetic boys and one girl. Mary had inherited both money and land from her father, and with her money and John's work it seems that the Shakespeares were able to give their children a good life. William received at least a basic education at the King Edward VI School in his hometown, where he studied subjects like reading, writing, poetry, history, Latin, and Greek.

The town of Stratford-upon-Avon wasn't very large – only about 1,500 people lived there. And the main trade was in livestock. So in many ways the people of London thought that nothing good or impressive could ever come out of Stratford.

But boy were they wrong.

In 1568, when William was just four years old, there was a big change in England that affected his family.

Catholic Queen Mary I of England died, and her sister Elizabeth I - who was a Protestant and who had been a prisoner for her faith – became Queen. Once they heard the news, Catholics across the country (including William's family) grew very afraid. They remembered how severe Mary I had been with people who didn't support her religion, and now it seemed that the tables had turned. Now it seemed that Elizabeth was in a position to get revenge and to start punishing Catholics.

It was in this climate of religious uncertainty and outbreaks of the plague that William Shakespeare grew up and received his education. His life is pretty well documented from birth all the way through school, but in 1578, at the age of 14, William Shakespeare finished school and disappeared from history – and he didn't appear again for approximately four years.

Piecing together Shakespeare's youth is kind of like a treasure hunt and a puzzle: historians must rely on documents that somehow managed to survive destruction and getting lost over several hundred years. And while there are no shortage of theories about what William may have been doing during those missing four years (working for his father, learning a new trade, running from religious persecution), no one can be too sure.

All that anyone can say with certainty is that on November 28, 1582 William appears again in the public record when, at the tender young age of 18, he got married to a woman named Anne Hathaway who was eight years older than him. Seven months later, there is a birth certificate with William and Anne's names on it. Doing the math, and knowing that a baby needs nine months to grow, researchers have come to the obvious conclusion that Anne was two months pregnant when they got married.

This fact has made some historians think that William may have been forced into marrying a girl that he had gotten pregnant. And as the later years of their marriage would show, it's possible that William and Anne were never really in love but had been forced to spend the rest of their lives married to each other.

William and Anne's first child was a daughter and they named her Susanna. Less than two years later, William and Anne welcomed twins into their family and named them after some close friends: the boy was named Hamnet and the girl was named Judith.

Both girls would live long and happy lives and would outlive their father William, but sadly young Hamnet would get sick and die tragically at the age of 11, which meant that the Shakespeare name did not live on after William died (his brothers never had any children).

After the birth of his twins, William Shakespeare disappeared one more time from the historical record – and this time the mystery period lasted for some seven years (until the year 1592). What was Shakespeare doing during those years? Had he gotten into trouble and did he have to run away? Was he learning more about writing

4   Image   source:
http://en.wikipedia.org/wiki/Anne_Hathaway_(Shakespeare's_wife)

plays (as far as we know, he never went to university, so he had to learn how to write somewhere).

Whatever may have happened after his twins were born, when he appeared again in 1592, Shakespeare was living in London and performing with an acting troupe called Lord Chamberlain's Men.

What in the world could have transpired from the time when Shakespeare was living a quiet family life in Stratford-upon-Avon to the time he was working with a travelling group of actors? While no one can be too sure, it seems that the acting troupe Lord Chamberlain's Men may have been on a trip visiting villages across the country, and one of their trips took them through Stratford-upon-Avon at some point. Perhaps it was during one of these trips that William was able to meet some of the players and spend time with them.

By this time, Shakespeare had written a collection of sonnets (poems) that would later be published without his permission. Was it this ability to write beautiful poetry that captured the attention of the travelling actors and their backers? What was it about this young family man that caught the eye of the acting troupe? Did he impress them with his writing skills or did he possibly act out some scenes with them? However it happened, Shakespeare managed to get an invitation from Lord Chamberlain's Men to join them, and soon he left his family in Stratford-upon-Avon and went on the road as a touring actor.

Back then, actors weren't famous and well-respected like they are today. In fact, actors were looked at as men who didn't have a real job. Even though they worked hard preparing for their shows, most actors didn't make a lot of money, and they certainly weren't well-liked by most members of the community. They were accused of keeping real people from doing their jobs.

Instead of being like modern actors who are independent contractors that work one job at a time, back in Shakespeare's time, actors worked for "troupes" that were financed by wealthy individuals. In each troupe, there would be a leading man, several character actors, a comedian, and generally one or two younger actors who would play the parts of the woman (there were no female actresses back then). Each troupe would also have a writer to prepare unique plays, and the men would be responsible for organizing all the details of each new production.

Shakespeare seems to have mainly worked behind the scenes, although from time to time he did play roles in plays that he wrote himself, and in those written by other people. But it wasn't long before William became famous for what he could do with a pen. Both as a writer and possibly as an editor, it is no wonder that Shakespeare found his home in the theater world making people laugh, cry, and think about the important issues of the day.

By the time Shakespeare appeared again in the public record in 1592 (when he was listed as a part of Lord Chamberlain's Men), the culture of England had changed a lot. Queen Elizabeth – while occasionally punishing traitors or those who tried to promote the Catholic Church – tried her best not to stir up trouble for the people of her nation. She wanted to support a peaceful atmosphere where the arts could flourish and where her citizens could enjoy the finer things in life, which for her included going to the theater.

Elizabeth I invited Shakespeare and Lord
Chamberlain's Men to perform at her palace and
it wasn't long she became a public fan of him
and his work. No doubt, this support from the
throne helped Shakespeare to feel more
confident about his work and helped his
reputation to rise above that of most other
playwrights and actors.

---

[5] Image   source:
http://en.wikipedia.org/wiki/Elizabeth_I_of_England

The career of William Shakespeare seems to have begun rather suddenly: just a few years elapsed from the time when he was a young father who wrote poetry in his spare time to the time he started working as an inexperienced actor in a troupe.

But now that he was beginning to get some recognition and even acting for the Queen, would he be able to live up to all the expectations others had for him? His early plays *The Two Gentlemen of Verona* and *The Taming of the Shrew* were comedies and showed some potential, but could Shakespeare grow as a writer and tackle more dramatic source material? Could he support his wife and children back in Stratford-upon-Avon with the money he made in London, and could he avoid angering the powerful people in charge of England? Would his work last beyond his death?

After getting work with Lord Chamberlain's Men and moving to London, Shakespeare would have to keep working hard to prove his worth and to live his dream as a playwright.

Chapter 2: The Career of William Shakespeare

Sometime after getting married, William Shakespeare began to write down his thoughts in the form of poetry. Apparently he never meant for anyone to read most of what he wrote, because he included some very personal thoughts in his sonnets. There were many poems about love, and several historians think that Shakespeare may have even been in love with the "fair youth" that he wrote about.

Even though Shakespeare would have probably preferred to keep most of these poems to himself, in 1609 a publishing company somehow got hold of Shakespeare's work and printed many copies for people to buy. Even though he was upset, Shakespeare didn't take any legal action to stop them.

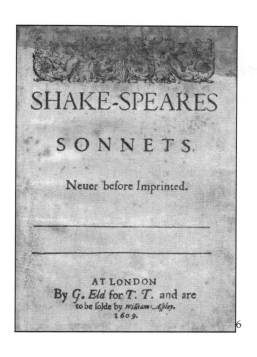

6

Shortly after reappearing in the pages of history in London as he performed with Lord Chamberlain's Men, Shakespeare began to take his plays more seriously. Most of his early works were either historical or comedies, and, although his works showed a lot of promise there is no doubt that Shakespeare wasn't a born genius. Like anyone else, he had to become good at what he did, and he needed the help of experienced writers. But more than anything, Shakespeare

---

[6] Image source: http://en.wikipedia.org/wiki/Shakespeare's_sonnets

just needed some practice – something he got plenty of by writing play after play after play.

Mainly basing their opinions on the quality of the work, some historians think that *The Two Gentlemen of Verona* was among Shakespeare's first written and published plays. They note that there was a very small cast in the play (making it easier to write), and that some of the scenes where there are more than two characters show that the writer did not know of many techniques used for writing successful stage plays.

But aside from looking at the quality of a play, historians trying to put together the puzzle of William Shakespeare's life's work have to pay attentions to details like when the play was first performed, when it was first printed, and what kinds of historical references are included within each one. The very first plays that can firmly be attributed to Shakespeare are *Henry VI* parts I to III, which deal with the life and times of a former King of England. Famous writer Thomas Nashe may have helped Shakespeare to craft his first play (part II), and to become a more successful playwright.

Shakespeare's acting troupe "Lord Chamberlain's Men" began performing the plays that Shakespeare was writing around 1590-1591, and it wasn't long before this young writer starting getting credit for his wonderful work. After writing several historical plays and then some comedies (like *The Taming of the Shrew*) later on, Shakespeare noticed that the people of England were less interested in comedy and more in drama. So somewhere around 1594-1595, Shakespeare prepared one of his most famous and enduring plays - *Romeo and Juliet*, followed shortly after by *The Merchant of Venice*.

Shakespeare was invited to perform his plays before Queen Elizabeth on more than one occasion, and later he went to the palace of her

[7] Image source: http://en.wikipedia.org/wiki/Romeo_and_Juliet

successor, King James I, and performed several plays for him and his court – including (as we saw in the introduction)the famed play *The Merchant of Venice*. This latter play was especially famous for its speech by a hated Jewish moneylender. In a time when Jews were despised and treated as second-class citizens, Shakespeare wrote the following words:

> I am a Jew. Hath
> not a Jew eyes? Hath not a Jew hands, organs,
> dimensions, senses, affections, passions? fed with
> the same food, hurt with the same weapons, subject
> to the same diseases, healed by the same means,
> warmed and cooled by the same winter and summer, as
> a Christian is? If you prick us, do we not bleed?
> if you tickle us, do we not laugh?

In this speech, the Jewish character (Shylock) forces the audience to think deeply about the fact that people of Jewish heritage are humans too. Even though they speak a different language, look different, and have different customs, that does not mean that any person has a right to mistreat or prejudge a Jewish person.

This was a completely new thought. Whereas other writers may have used the character of Shylock to make people laugh, Shakespeare used the character to make people examine some of the deepest prejudices they had.

In fact, at the end of the speech Shylock talks about getting revenge for being treated so badly. And who does he say taught him about revenge? He blames Christians. So Shakespeare gave a second lesson to his audience: don't say you are a Christian with your mouth and then turn around and do unchristian things (like getting revenge) when you think no one is looking. Many people in England were guilty of trying to get revenge for the way Mary I had treated Catholics, but Shakespeare knew that this was a terrible thing to do.

It was the ability to write an entertaining story that caused the audience to think that made Shakespeare such an outstanding writer.

Shortly before starting work on a special play for King James I, Shakespeare's acting troupe found themselves in a pretty tough position. They had been using their own venue for plays (which they simply called "The Theatre"), and that venue had been built on land that the troupe rented from a local wealthy businessman. In 1597, the owner decided that he no longer wanted to rent his land out to the actors, and that when the contract with them had expired, he was going to take the land back for his own use.

Worst of all, this wealthy man told the actors that since they had built their theater on his land, the building that they had been using for several years would become his property as well. In other words, the actors would not have a place to put on their shows; their careers would be over and Lord Chamberlain's Men would have to break up.

The actors could not reason with the landowner, and things looked bleak for the troupe. True to his word, the wealthy businessman (whose name was Giles Allen) kicked the actors off his property the next year and did not them have access to The Theatre.

All may have seemed lost for some time, but when Giles went away to his country home for Christmas, a sudden opportunity presented itself, and the actors saw a way to get back what was rightfully theirs. Together with some friends, the troupe snuck onto the property of Giles and The Theatre and completely disassembled the structure, taking the wood with them and leaving the land completely bare. The actors didn't feel like they were doing anything wrong - after all, they were the ones who had bought the building materials with their own hard-earned money. The troupe stored the wood in a warehouse near the Thames River, and as soon as they got the opportunity they snuck the materials to the other side and used them to build a theater of their own, which they called "The Globe Theater".

The Globe Theater used a fascinating construction method that gave the building about 20 sides and three floors of seating. Because everyone with a seat was at different heights and arranged in a kind of circle, everyone could have a good view of the show.

But oddly enough, the best seats in the house were also the cheapest. Most poor people would buy the standing-room only seats on the floor (these folks were called "groundlings") while middle and upper class workers were the ones who could afford to sit higher up. It was mainly men that attended the plays (remember that the theater wasn't a respectable place for ladies yet), and if the audience didn't like what they saw then they would have no problem yelling at the performers, and even throwing rotten food at them. But if the show was good, then those same people would yell and shout about how much they loved the play.

The stage had a trap door in the floor and in the ceiling, and the background was painted, making the show look very realistic and making people look like they were going underground or up into the sky. The stage actually stretched forward into the audience so that a lot of the acting happened just inches away from the spectators. There was a live orchestra hidden above the stage, and for some productions, cannons loaded with blanks could be fired (one of these cannons misfired in 1613 and actually burned the theater to the ground; it was rebuilt the next year).

8

These were the golden years of Shakespeare. Each new play brought crowds of people to the

8 Image source: http://en.wikipedia.org/wiki/Globe_Theatre

theater where he was a part owner. And because he received a portion of the ticket sales, Shakespeare soon found that he had plenty of money in his pockets.

After James I became King of England in 1603, the nation that Shakespeare lived in began to change. Before becoming King of England, James had even gone so far as to believe that some women in Scotland were witches, and that they should be tortured and executed, but by the time he sat on the throne in England, his views had softened.

Even so, there were doubts about what would happen to the religious culture of the country. James was a Protestant, but his mother died a Catholic, and it was rumored that his wife (Queen Anne of Denmark) was also a Catholic. Even though King James worked hard to promote the same peaceful climate that Elizabeth had promoted, there were still some people who wanted to take James off of the throne and replace him with someone else.

But King James and his religion weren't the only things on the minds of England - the makeup of the population itself had changed in the years since Elizabeth had died. Instead of being mostly men and women born and raised in England, many Scottish people had moved to the south to be a part of the new United Kingdom. While new culture might look good on paper, the fact is that some people didn't like the way that their new neighbors from the North talked and acted. In fact, many Englishmen made fun of their new fellow citizens, and even of the King himself (who was from Scotland).

Would Shakespeare join in and make fun of the King for being from a different country? How would he handle the issue of witchcraft and religion?

Because King James I was a supporter of Shakespeare's acting troupe, to show their appreciation and respect for the King, the actors changed the name of their group from "Lord Chamberlain's Men" to "The King's Men". It appears that in some private moment between the two men, King James asked Shakespeare to write a play just for him and his court. Shakespeare had previously done this favor for Queen Elizabeth I, so it wasn't unheard of. But whether or not the King personally asked him to do so, Shakespeare set out to write a play with the King in mind, and he did a wonderful job when he wrote the play *Macbeth*.

9

Because he wrote the play during such a turbulent time in England, and because he had the King in mind when he did so, Shakespeare made sure to include a lot of details that concerned the everyday citizen of England, along with some hidden messages aimed directly at the King.

The fact that there was instability in the country was something that Shakespeare included in

Macbeth. Knowing that the King had been concerned at one time with witches, Shakespeare wrote a scene where the main character was told his future by a group of three witches. He also described a country where no one was sure about their new leader, and this seemed to appeal to Shakespeare's audience.

But Shakespeare went even further, and modern scholars think that a plot against the government influences Shakespeare's writing of *Macbeth*. Shortly before the play was performed for King James, there was a terrible conspiracy against his life that almost killed him and his political advisors.

Known as the "Gunpowder Plot", the conspiracy was organized by a group of Catholic Englishmen (including Guy Fawkes) who gathered 36 barrels of gunpowder together with the goal of blowing up the English Parliament building (called the House of Lords) as the King gave an important speech. All of the important politicians of England – including the King – would have been blown to pieces on November 5, 1605 if an anonymous tip had not led investigators to Guy Fawkes as he hid beneath the House of Lords and guarded the barrels.

Knowing that there were some in the audience who may have known about the conspiracy (or who may have even been a part of it) Shakespeare made sure to include some information in his new play about the dangers of killing a king. The main character in the play (named Macbeth) does just that, and his life went downhill and the entire nation suffered because of his thirst for power. This detail in the plot was a kind of secret message to anyone in the audience, telling them that killing James I would not lead to anything good for England.

The play included words of praise for the current king, and it put a good character in the play who was thought to be an ancestor of James and said that James and his relatives would rule England and other countries for a very long time.

Shakespeare knew how to write a play. Instead of just writing scenes that would entertain people, he tried to have his characters talk about the things that were on the minds of the audience. In *Macbeth*, he put the newly enthroned King James in a favorable light and warned those who might want to hurt the King. But at the same time he included something for James to think about – Macbeth started down his dark road when he listened to the bad ideas of his wife and did what she wanted without thinking. The lesson for King James would be to not let his Catholic wife stir up trouble for the nation.

Shakespeare worked very hard, and during the prime part of his career he wrote an average of 2 plays per year. Money was flowing so much that Shakespeare was able to get an apartment in London for himself, and in 1597 he bought a very expensive house for his wife and children back in Stratford-upon-Avon. Shakespeare's wife Anne never left the small town she and William grew up in, and it seems that William spent most of his time in London writing and performing plays.

But at least once a year – normally during the religious celebration of Lent (the six week period leading up to Easter) – the theaters in London all closed their doors and the actors took a sort of vacation from their jobs. During this forced vacation, Shakespeare would regularly make the journey back to Stratford-upon-Avon to spend time with his family. Aside from sending them money during the year, it seems that Shakespeare truly enjoyed his annual trip to see and be with his children.

Some historians have noticed that Shakespeare and his wife seemed to have a strained relationship. Maybe it was the age difference and maybe it was because Shakespeare had been forced into marrying Anne (she had been pregnant with his child at the time), but whatever the reason it didn't seem that the two adults really wanted to be around each other. If anything, they tolerated each other mainly because of the children (and because it was difficult to get divorced back then).

This husband and wife spent most of their time separated from each other, and when William's son Hamnet died in 1596, it's possible that Shakespeare wasn't even there to say goodbye to him.

But no matter what, it's clear that Shakespeare's personal life was not what gave him satisfaction. He was a writer, and he wanted to be remembered for the plays that he wrote. He spent time with royalty, and his words could make entire nations think about their actions and how things should be done.

As Shakespeare focused his career more on dramas, his reputation as a playwright only got better, and it seemed like things would never change for "the Bard (poet) from Avon".

But like all good things, Shakespeare's life and career were coming to an end – much sooner than anyone expected them to.

Chapter 3: The Late Life of William Shakespeare

While Shakespeare continued writing comedies for some time after his beloved son Hamnet died, it is likely that this great personal tragedy gave greater depth when he decided later on to focus on writing dramatic plays. Plays like *Othello*, *King Lear*, and *Antony and Cleopatra* were tragedies where the story did not have a happy ending, and while some people may think that these plays were a reflection of Shakespeare's own sad life, it is probably closer to the truth to say that Shakespeare was simply giving the audience what they wanted. When the people wanted to see plays about historical fiction of funny situations, Shakespeare wrote plays along those lines. But once tastes changed and comedies were no longer as popular as they once were, Shakespeare stopped writing so many comedies, and turned his attention to drama.

Shakespeare's last play was titled *Two Noble Kinsmen*, and it was written around 1612-1613 together with fellow playwright John Fletcher (who took over Shakespeare's position with The King's Men once Shakespeare stopped writing).

Around this time, William Shakespeare decided that he had done everything that he wanted to in the world of the theater. In a time when many people died in their 30s and 40s, Shakespeare was nearly 50 years old, and had been writing plays for at least 20 years. He was rich, and now he felt that it was time for him to go home to Stratford-upon-Avon and live the quiet life of a retired man.

When Shakespeare arrived back home to his large house, he found that things had quieted down over the years. Of course his youngest son had died, his oldest daughter Susana had already left home to get married to a doctor, and his remaining daughter Judith was engaged to marry a wine dealer.

But in March of 1616, it was clear that Shakespeare was having some serious health problems and he started to think seriously about what would happen after he died. William didn't like the man that Judith was about to marry (he had caused a scandal in town during their engagement) and so practically on his deathbed Shakespeare altered his will to make sure that the bulk of his money went to Susana and any male children she should have.

One month later, William Shakespeare died on his birthday – April 23, 1616 – probably of a serious fever (like the outbreaks of typhus that were attacking the people of England that year). In his will, he left gifts to friends and family, but then made sure that his lawyers added one very strange sentence to the document that has puzzled historians down to this day. In his Last Will and Testament, Shakespeare hardly mentioned his wife Anne – but he did have this to say:

"Item, I give unto my wife my second best bed with the furniture."

Why would he only leave a bed to his wife – and his second best bed at that? While some scholars may think that Shakespeare was trying to insult his wife one final time (there is no doubt that the two had a very strange relationship), others think that perhaps the puzzling note was one final romantic comment from a husband to his wife.

Is there any evidence to help us solve this final puzzle from the life of Shakespeare?

Many researchers have pointed out the fact that, as William's wife, Anne would automatically receive one-third of her husband's property. Her needs would be taken care of. So anything that a husband specifically left to his wife in his Last Will and Testament would probably be something very special for the two of them.

In a time where it was a very important duty to give a family's guests the best of, the best bed of the house would naturally be set aside for guests. This meant that the "second best bed" of most English houses would be the one shared by the husband and wife in the master bedroom. Perhaps by leaving his wife his "second best bed", Shakespeare was encouraging her to think of the happy times they had shared during their marriage. Instead of being an insult, perhaps the line was a love note from the grave to the wife who had supported her husband in his career throughout the decades.

Shakespeare was buried in the Holy Trinity Church in his hometown, and strangely enough the world did not seem to notice.

10

It is important to note that Shakespeare had been out of the theater world for some time, and most people still saw his plays onstage in the years after he died. But when a fellow actor and close friend of Shakespeare, Richard Burbage, died in 1619, the world stopped and mourned him. Burbage had played the title role in many of Shakespeare's plays, and when he died then the world finally realized what had been lost. In a time before the internet and easy research tools, Burbage was the public face of all the hard work that Shakespeare had done behind the scenes. When the source of the plays disappeared, it was hard for the average person to grasp the loss. But

[10] Image source: http://commons.wikimedia.org/wiki/File:Shakespeare-Tomb-Stratford.jpg

when the man who had brought many of Shakespeare's characters to life (including Hamlet, Othello, and King Lear) died, it was clear that an era had ended and that the theater would never be the same.

In 1623, William Shakespeare's plays were released for the first time in a collection called the *First Folio*. A little over 100 years later (in Victorian England), there was a tremendous resurgence of interest in Shakespeare's plays. Irish playwright George Bernard Shaw made fun of this sudden and intense interest, calling it "Bardolatry" - or "Idolatry and Worship of the Bard". He felt that Shakespeare was a good author, but that he should have written more about the social issues of his day (as Shaw did with his plays). But despite the comments of critics like Shaw, most people were thrilled to rediscover the writings of Shakespeare. To this day, his works are performed all over the world in all the major languages.

Around the time that Shakespeare became popular again, some very outspoken scholars began to think that maybe William Shakespeare did not write all of the plays with his name on them. They think that maybe a member of the royal court or another writer simply hid behind the name of William Shakespeare and wrote the plays themselves. What are their reasons for making these claims?

1. Of the few times where William Shakespeare's name is recorded on official documents, there are different spellings of it. This fact (along with the fact that no handwritten letters from Shakespeare still exist) make some researchers think that maybe William Shakespeare could barely read and write - let alone have a vocabulary of some 20,000 words, which was very impressive for its time.
2. Shakespeare wrote about a wide variety of subjects, and could use the right words when talking about legal situations, hunting, sailing, and life in the royal court.
3. When he died, there was no mention of books or manuscripts among his many belongings that he left to his family. Researchers have been unable to find any books owned by Shakespeare in the libraries surrounding Stratford-upon-Avon.
4. Shakespeare did not have an impressive formal education.

Despite these arguments, the majority of scholars who have closely studied the historical documents and works attributed to Shakespeare see no reason to doubt that he really was the author. Looking at the same information as the critics, most researchers come to a very different conclusion.

1. They have seen that the majority of times that Shakespeare's name was signed, it was done so by clerks and lawyers and not by Shakespeare himself. That might explain some of the spelling differences.
2. Shakespeare may have had co-writers and researchers help him with some of the more technical and detailed parts of his plays (or he may have simply researched them himself).
3. In the First Folio – the collection of Shakespeare's works published in 1623 – the actors from Shakespeare's own troupe who put the collection together give him the writing credit for the 36 plays in the collection.
4. The education shouldn't be a big issue, because other famous writers of the time (like Christopher Marlowe) also did not have an impressive formal education. But no one doubts Marlowe's writing, so why should they doubt Shakespeare?

Perhaps more than anything else, Shakespeare's critics of his day prove his authorship. In 1592 fellow playwright Robert Greene called Shakespeare "and upstart crow", and in 1594 he is listed as an actor performing for the Queen.

So no matter what some very impressive scholars might say about the works of William Shakespeare, there is no good reason to think that he did not write the plays we attribute to him (at least 37 plays altogether). The facts show that Shakespeare was a poet and playwright who was born and raised in Stratford-upon-Avon, and who died in his home in that same town. Even though he was just a boy from a small town, we need to fight the temptation to fill in the blanks of his life with conspiracies and secret identities. The facts point to one conclusion: William Shakespeare wrote what we think he wrote and was as great as we think he was.

Chapter 4: What's So Great About Shakespeare?

The man born as William Shakespeare singlehandedly changed writing and the English language for everyone who came after him. His works added words to the language he wrote in, he was a master of storytelling, and some four hundred years later, audiences are still crying at the dramas that he wrote and laughing at his comedies. In a time where actors and the theater were not taken seriously, Shakespeare became a national treasure and showed that the theater could be a place to examine social issues as well as a place to be entertained.

The theater where Shakespeare wrote and performed many of his most successful plays burned to the ground after a cannon misfired and was rebuilt the next year. But the theater was closed once again in 1642 when the Puritans convinced everybody that the theater was a place for offensive shows, and that nothing good would come from people going there.

Eventually the original site of the Globe Theater was built over, and when in 1997 a new version of the famous theater was built, the new owners had to build it some distance away from the original. Today, tourists can walk around in the open-roofed theater and imagine what the original venue may have been like, and they can even see plays that are put on from time to time.

Since Shakespeare died, there have been countless productions of his works, including movies released on TV and in theaters. Students in schools and universities around the word study his words and writing style, and researchers still work hard to track down some "lost works" of Shakespeare that might be buried in the back of a museum or library.

William Shakespeare spent his life writing. But instead of writing about himself, he focused on creating characters who had feelings and motivations that his audience could identify with. He didn't leave letters or a diary where he talked about his own problems and struggles in life – even though he surely had plenty. Instead, the only writings Shakespeare left behind are poems and plays that we all can identify with and that we will pass on to the next generation.

The measure of a person's greatness is seen by how they affect others. Shakespeare can easily be classed as one of the greatest humans ever to live. His words have been appreciated by millions, and many others have started acting, directing, producing, and writing because of his influence.

William Shakespeare's private life may be a puzzle in many ways, but his career as a playwright is a shared heritage that the entire human race can enjoy.

5578000R00032

Printed in Germany
by Amazon Distribution
GmbH, Leipzig